Red Bird

BY ALYSSA KREKELBERG

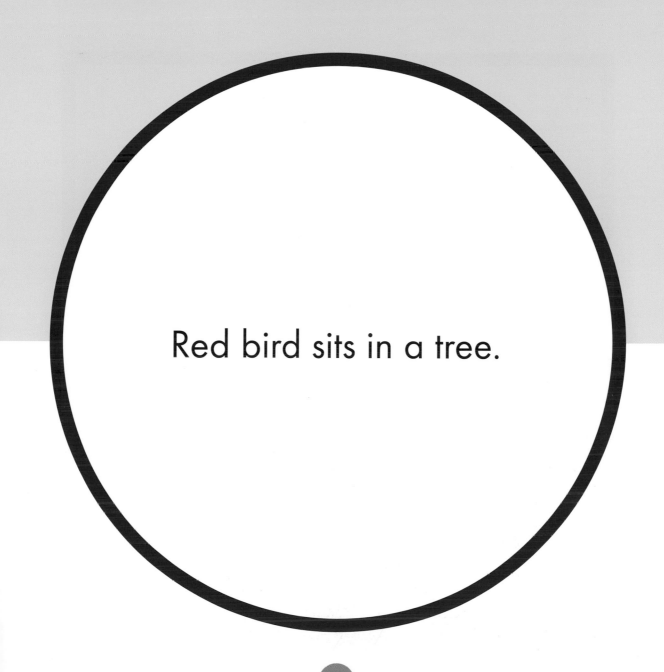

Red bird sits in a tree.

Red bird looks for food.

Red bird eats birdseed.

Red bird looks at the squirrel.

Red bird plays in the water.

Red bird comes to the window.

Red bird sits by yellow flowers.

Red bird flies over a tree.

Red bird finds its nest.

Red bird flies away.

Sight words are a foundation for reading. It's important for young readers to have sight words memorized at a glance without breaking them down into individual letter sounds. Sight words are often phonetically irregular and can't be sounded out, so readers need to memorize them. Knowing sight words allows readers to focus on more difficult words in the text. The intent of this book is to repeat specific sight words as many times as possible throughout the story. Through repetition of the words, emerging readers will recognize, and ideally memorize, each sight word. Memorizing sight words can help improve readers' literacy skills.

bird

red

23

About the Author

Alyssa Krekelberg is a children's book editor and author. She lives in Minnesota and enjoys exploring the great outdoors with her hyper husky.

The Child's World®
childsworld.com

Published by The Child's World®
1980 Lookout Drive • Mankato, MN 56003-1705
800-599-READ • www.childsworld.com

Photographs ©: Dennis W. Donohue/Shutterstock Images, cover, 1, 14; Merlin Halteman/Shutterstock Images, 2; iStockphoto, 5, 13, 17, 23; John Kotlowski/Shutterstock Images, 6; Alexander Sviridov/Shutterstock Images, 9; Jillian Cain/iStockphoto, 10; Shutterstock Images, 18; Bob Christian/iStockphoto, 21

ISBN 9781503835689
LCCN 2019943125

Printed in the United States of America